Chris

SHRINK WRAP

Keds &
Laughter is a Joy of Life!

Love Uncle Bob
xxx oo

Christmas 1992

SHRINK WRAP

Cartoons by
P. S. MUELLER

SPECTACLE LANE PRESS

Published by
Spectacle Lane Press, Box 34, Georgetown, CT 06829
ISBN 0-930753-12-7

Published simultaneously in the United States and Canada.
Printed in the United States of America.

Dedicated to the Memory of
Goffrey Hughes

We won't see another like him.

MUELLER ON MUELLER

A strange career choice, cartooning. No one can really TEACH you how to do it. There's no apprentice system for it. I guess you have to spend a lot of time alone in your room when you're a kid.

I spent many hours in my room, studying MAD Magazine and poring over my Dad's old copies of *The New Yorker*. I wanted to be James Thurber, Don Martin, and Saul Steinberg, but somehow I ended up as P.S. Mueller.

Teachers who confiscated my drawings were the first to learn I was a bit different. Sometimes, when they thought I was daydreaming, I was actually thinking up gags. When they thought I was dutifully taking notes, I was jotting down a goofy scenario. My grade school art teacher banished me to the hallway, forever, because I could never quite get with her regimen of pâpier-maché squirrels and tempera paint turkeys.

Somehow, I got all the way through high school and college without ever taking an art course. I think you'll agree—it shows. But all the way through high school and college I was out in the hallway, drawing, slowly developing a style no one else would want to call their own.

I started publishing my odd, little graphic notions over twenty years ago. Various careers didn't get in the way, though they occasionally slowed my output. I worked in restaurants, bowling alleys, and greenhouses, and eventually spent quite a number of years as a disc jockey. But, like so many times before, when the record was ending and the news was standing by, I was out in the hallway drawing cartoons.

Eight years ago I realized I wasn't fit for much else and went at it full time. Now I'm forty and I have a new book for you to look at, the product of many strange turns of phrase and dreadful ideas. Some people come out of the closet. I came out of the hallway.

"OH LOOK! HE'S LEARNED SOMETHING NEW!"

GOOD GUMS.

BAD GUMS.

A HEDGE AGAINST REALITY.

DESIGNATED HITLER.

EPSOM AND HIS SALTS.

12

13

EVOLUTION + REAL ESTATE

THE FIRST CONFLICT.

MUELLER

A DECADE OF HAIR.

MUELLER

18

INFORMATION   THE SILENT KILLER.

MUELLER

21

23

MOVEMENT.

THE POETRY.

THE PROSE.

MUELLER

A TOTAL ECLIPSE OF THE FUN.

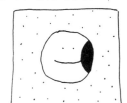
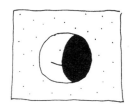
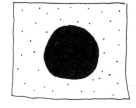

P.S. MUELLER

IRRITANTS

POLLEN.

CHEMICALS.

BIFF.

BUFFY.

MUELLER

CHILD CUSTODY SUIT.

MUELLER

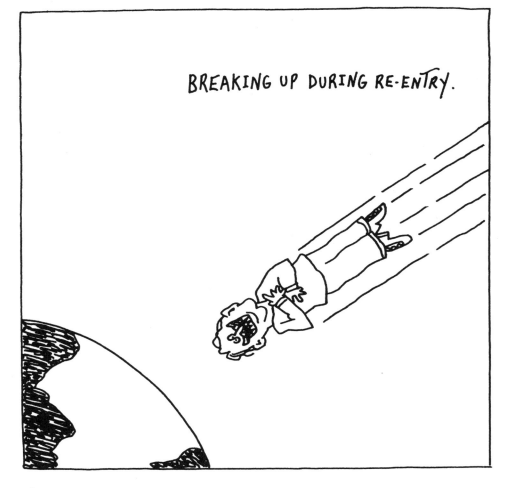

BREAKING UP DURING RE-ENTRY.

MUELLER

EMPTY-V.

MUELLER

MUELLER

WAITING FOR THAT FIRST CUP OF COFFEE.

MUELLER

33

RAMBLING EXCUSE.

MUELLER

34

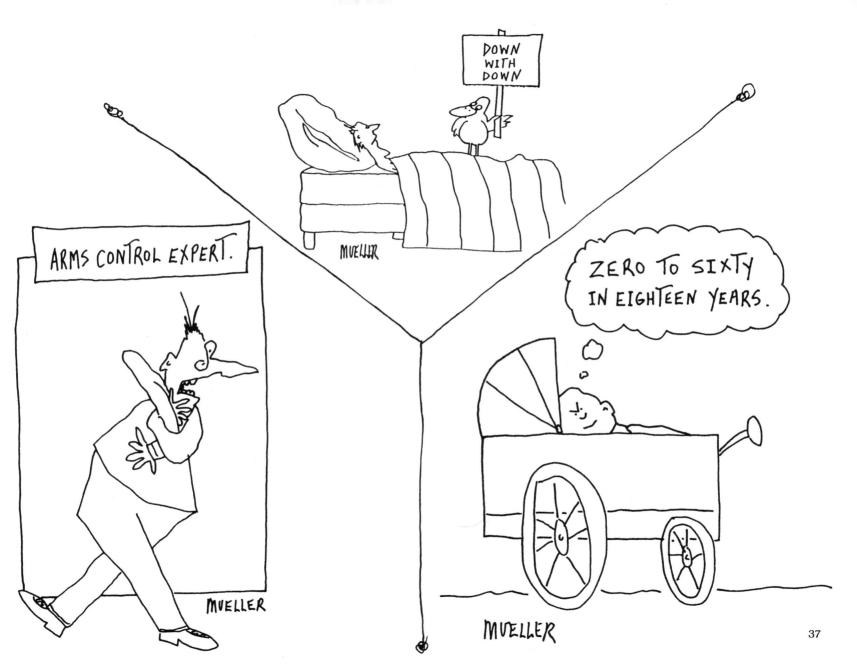

NATURE IS A GREAT RECYCLER.

39

ICARUS SPRAY

MUELLER

THE CONVERSION OF ST. BERNARD.

MUELLER

IRON PLUS +

MUELLER

MUELLER

A CUP OF COFFEE DRINKS A MAN.

HUNDREDS OF GOOD REASONS NOT TO INHALE.

FUNDAMENTALIST DIRT WORSHIP.

THE TOMB OF THE UNKNOWN NOBODY.

51

ANOTHER FLATLANDER GOES BAD.

JUST PLAIN FOLKS

THE BOXED SET.

MUELLER

MUELLER

54

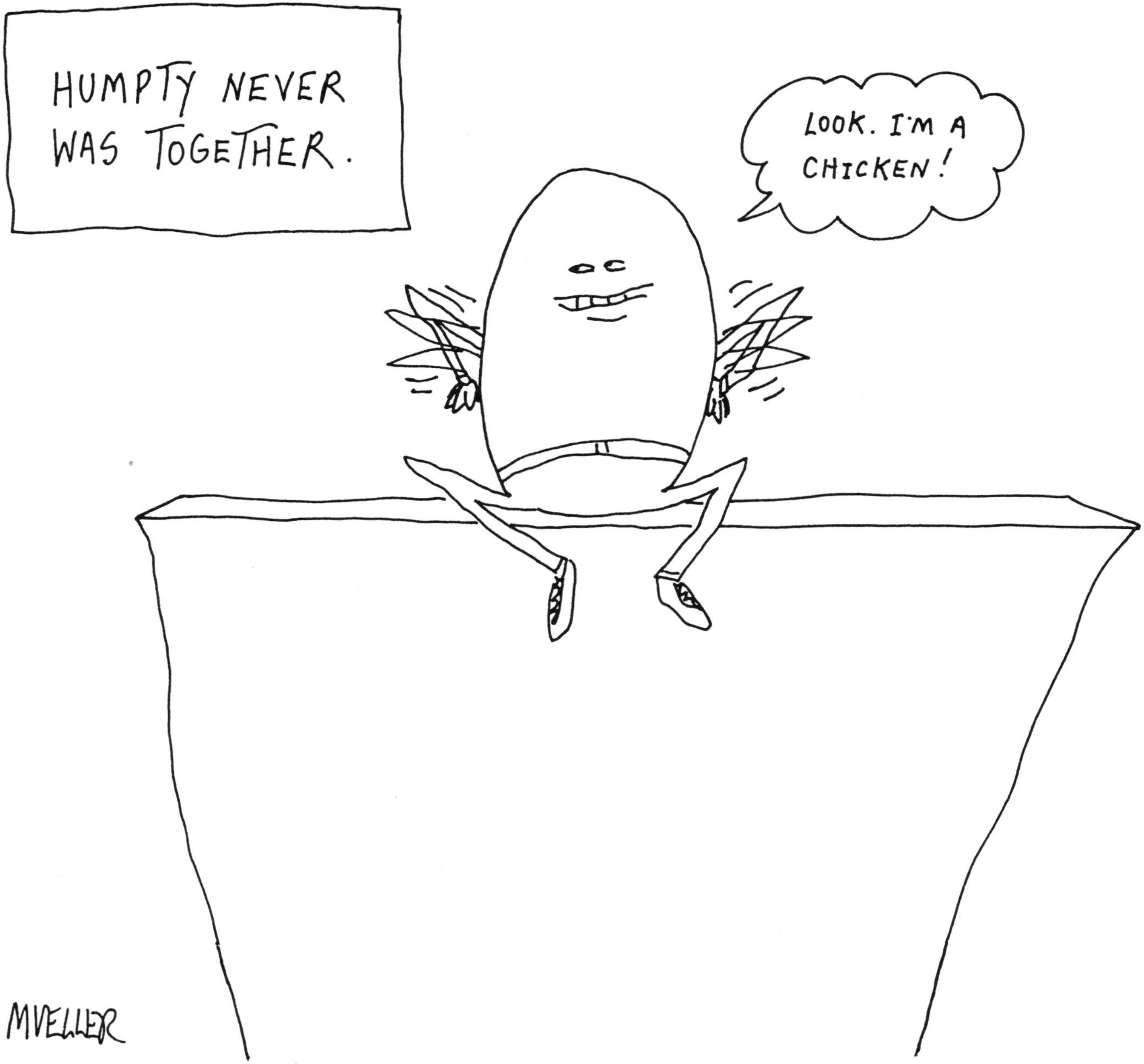
HUMPTY NEVER WAS TOGETHER.
LOOK. I'M A CHICKEN!
MUELLER

58

63

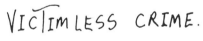

VICTIMLESS CRIME.

BEFORE WAFFLES THERE WAS NO GUILT.

HOUNDED BY A HOSTILE PRESS.

PRESSED BY A HOSTILE HOUND.

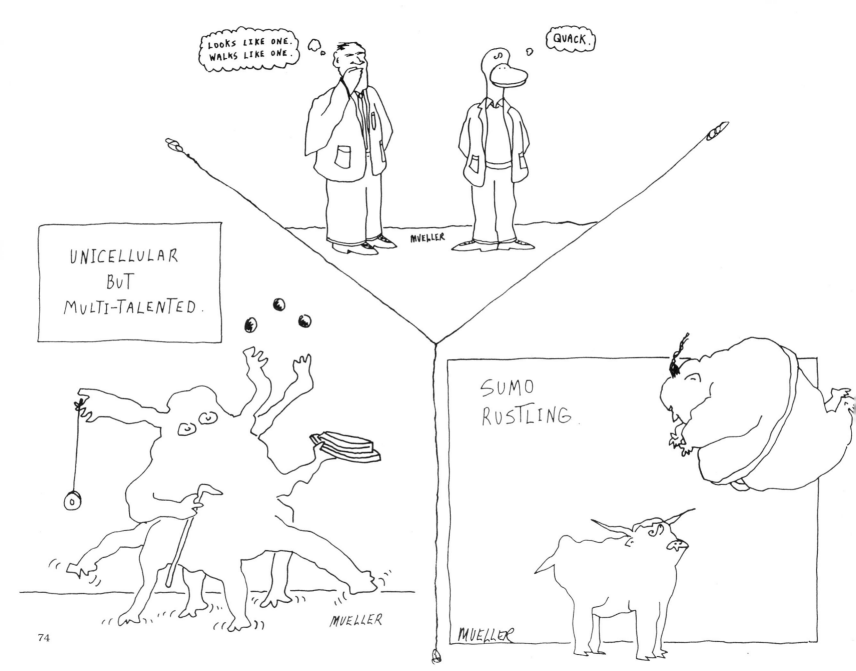

77

80

WHEN HELL FREEZES OVER.
TIME TO GO HOME.
MUELLER
NO NICHE.
MUELLER

83

BORN UNDER A BAD SIGN.

THE LOSS OF INNOCENCE.

THE TREE OF INFO-TAINMENT.

93

ON THE RANGE.
IT'S QUITE A LOT, BUT WE CALL IT HOME.
MUELLER

SHOULD I SIGN IT?
MUELLER

EXTREMELY DIFFERENTLY ABLED.

99

THE NEW WAVE.

MUELLER

MEN WORKING

MEN TALKING SPORTS

MUELLER

HIPPOCRATIC OAFS.

MUELLER

TROUBLE IN THE OZONE LAYER.

WHAT'S YOUR SIGN?

GOTTA BUILD SOME SHELVES.

MUELLER

THE GOD OF WHAT-NOTS AND BRIC-A-BRAC.

THE PLACEBO KID.

BANG.

MUELLER

VOODUNIT?

OATMEAL CAN'T DEFEND ITSELF.

THE RETURN OF THE PRODIGAL TOMATO.

108

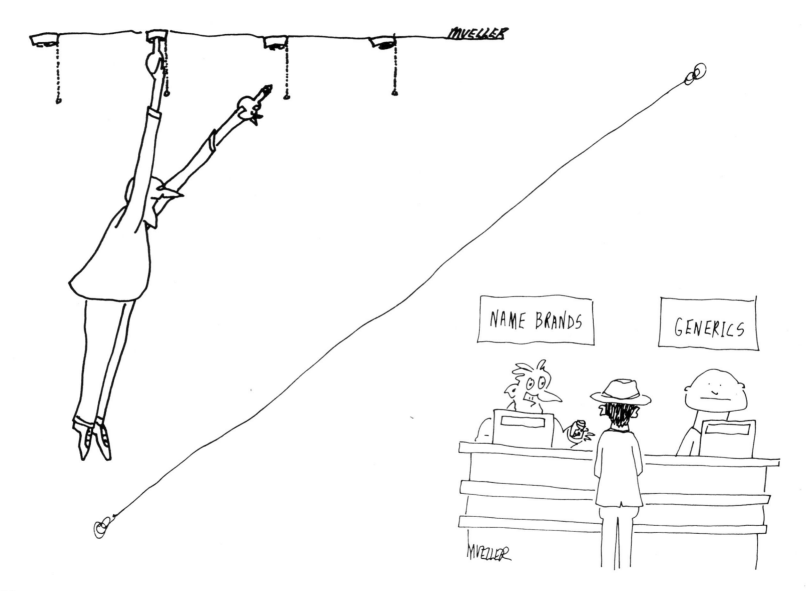

NAME BRANDS

GENERICS

120

121

HOW GRAVITY GETS EVEN.

FREE MONEY

MUELLER

MORE THAN JUST A PENCIL PUSHER.

JANE FONDA'S COOKOUT.

NO BARGAINING POSITION

FLAVOR ENHANCED ASPIRIN.

"YOU DON'T HAVE TO BE A ROCKET SCIENTIST TO FIGURE THIS OUT, BUT IT HELPS."

SETTLED OUT OF COURT.

R.I.P.

R.I.P.

MUELLER

ORDER THESE LAUGH-LOADED HUMOR BOOKS TODAY!

BOOK TITLE	AUTHOR	DESCRIPTION	ORDER NUMBER	QUANTITY	PRICE	TOTAL
101 Ways to Dump on Your EX!	Oaky Miller	Getting even after divorce	0-930753-01-1		$5.95	
OperAntics	W. J. Brooke	Hilarious operatic spoof	0-930753-02-X		$7.95	
Things To Worry About	Len Cellla	Zany worries and phobias	0-930753-03-8		$6.95	
The Grandparents' Book	A. & S. Little	The light side of grandparenting	0-930753-04-6		$6.95	
How To Speak New Yorkese	J.Levine & N. Jackson	Daffy definitions of a strange language	0-930753--07-0		$6.95	
Stupid Stories	R.J. Leonard	Utterly silly stories for smart kids	0-930753-05-4		$5.95	
They're a Very Successful Family!	J. Farris	New Yorker cartoonist views the "burbs"	0-930753-08-9		$6.95	
College Slang 101	C. Eble	Undergraduates' underground language	0-930753-09--7		$5.95	
The Bumper Sticker Book	M. & D. Reilly	Highway humor in the fast lane	0-930753-10-0		$5.95	
Overtime	V. Iovino	A coach's advice to over-zealous parents	0-930753-06-2		$6.95	
The World According to Kids	H. Dunn	Wit and wisdom in the classroom	0-930753-11-9		$6.95	
Blinkies	A. Denny	Short poems and long laughs	1-879865-01-7		$6.95	
Here's Ronnie!	G. Melson	Nostalgic photo humor from the Reagan years	0-930753-00-3		$3.95	

SPECTACLE LANE PRESS
PO BOX 34. GEORGETOWN, CT 06829

Subtotal	
Shipping and handling	
Total paid	

ORDER FROM YOUR LOCAL BOOK STORE; OR FILL OUT AND SEND THIS ORDER BLANK ALONG WITH YOUR CHECK OR MONEY ORDER FOR THE TOTAL AMOUNT DUE TO SPECTACLE LANE PRESS, PO BOX 34, GEORGETOWN, CT. 06829

Add $2.50 shipping and handling for the first book and $.50 for each additional book. Add $2.00 more for books shipped to Canada. Overseas postage will be billed. Allow up to 4 weeks for delivery. Make check or money order payable to Spectacle Lane Press Inc. Connecticut residents add sales tax. Quantity discounts available upon request. Send book (s) to:

Name_____

Address_____

City_____ State_____ Zip_____